Cool Is
The Reaping

Best Wishes

Gordon Brennall

Cool Is
The Reaping

GORDON GREENALL

First Published 2008

Published by Gordon Greenall Associates
4 Park Road
Chipping Campden
Gloucestershire
GL55 6EA

Designed and realised by Loose Chippings Books
The Paddocks
Chipping Campden
Gloucestershire
GL55 6AU
www.loosechippings.org

Printed and bound in England

ISBN 978-0-9554217-2-3

**Gordon Greenall was diagnosed with
Chronic Lymphatic Leukaemia in May 2004**

This Leukaemia - he sees as a seamy disease
Darkening the white smoke of hope -
Turning down the light - less bright
(By the day) since it first spoke.
A snake biding time - waiting to strike
At he and his like -
A criminal bent on crime -
A ticking clock marking his time
Distorting the beat of bodily rhythms -
Sending organs into eventual schisms
As a billion dark lymphocytes - long gone astray -
Thoughtlessly take him over
Spilling more and more bile - till his life's washed away.

**But before that day
He hopes - with the proceeds from this book -
To contribute more
Towards research into a permanent cure.**

FOREWORD

It is my pleasure to write this Foreword to Gordon Greenall's second book of poems which he is publishing in aid of research into leukaemia.

This is a many-faceted illness of which we know both a great deal and far too little but research is progressing every day and very many people diagnosed with one or other form of leukaemia are alive and doing well today as a result. Some years ago two sons of a friend both died of the illness for which there was then no treatment. Today, they would have been alive and growing up thanks to the research which brought about a cure for this particular form of the illness.

Gordon Greenall has put his energy and commitment into writing a book as a leukaemia patient himself and buying and enjoying it is a way both of encouraging him and helping to fund more research which will, quite certainly, bring about more cures. Every penny really does count. Leukaemia may never be a preventable disease but one day it will assuredly be an eminently treatable and curable one.

I am delighted to commend Gordon's book to you.

Susan Hill
January 2008

Contents

Contents - *continued*

Line Drawings by Virginia Sandbach
Cover Photographs by Arthur Cunynghame

Autumn Fire

The morning shrouds of misty form
Cast by autumn clouds at muster
With mother-nature's moistening dew
Making damp - so we mistrust her.
The opened pores of August heat
And nostrils take the chill still air
Allowing those (cold) virus parasites
To produce a dose of ill will there.

So to sweep the chimney
And clear out the fire grate
With rods and brushes pushed
In through the soot door plate.
The airway of the chimney echoes
To the birds upon the thatch
Till their noise was muted
By smoke kindled with a match.

The musty smell of mildew damp
Is subject of poor opinion spoke -
Till words are overcome
By choking green wood smoke.
Paper turns to charcoal form
Giving off a vapour heat -
While a rhythmic living flame
Dances - to a crackling fruit-wood beat.

11

Familiar burning odours
And the warming fire place
Bring pleasure to a stuffy nose
And flush the pallid face.
Sparks fly from the dampish sticks
To singe the back of hairy hand
That puts more hardwood logs
On - a bed of last year's ashen sand.

The fire mouth draws a yellow life
Of sparks that hiss and roar
While the gold retriever dog
Lays head upon the flint-stone floor.
The indoor cat makes for the mat
But stops to preen her fur
Then gives the dog a painful nip
So that he must move for her.

More fresh axed blocks are
Stacked – on the burning flame.
A hot ember rolls upon the cat
For the dog to get the blame.
A pet tattoo then ensues
So the log-man has to intervene.
At which his wife rips into him
Saying, "Don't you be so mean".

Man and dog are in retreat
As they both have been ejected.
Off to the darkened potting shed
Feeling sad and sore neglected.
They light the ageing oil stove
And settle down to warming slumber.
Then they're ordered in again
To bring more fresh cut lumber.

Both man and dog agree
That women - they are cats,
They hiss and draw their claws
And appear like sonar guided bats.
So the decision it is made -
Man and dog will pay the club
And on the way they just may -
Take a warmer at the pub.

The Changing Countryside

The countryside I see today
Is not the like of yesterday.
The sight of cloth capped head
On body lean, or underfed.
The dialect from a Campden lip
Now rarely heard letting rip
A laborious profanity to us all
From across a dry stone wall.

Our farms have moved to wire fence
For stopping change a poor defence.
Foreign tongues in Campden fields
Spoke by Asian men, cropping yields.
I stand and listen with my doubts
But thankful they are picking sprouts
Cutting cabbage, corn or cauliflower
By the piece or by the hour.

Oil produced from foreign crops
With flowering blue and yellow tops
The linseed and the seeded rape
Grown to swell a central oil lake.
Foreign machines crushing seeds
Once considered foreign weeds
Then siphoned into giant tankers
Just to please those European bankers!

Imagine, Alec Cooper as an onion seller -
With his bike drinking in a bier keller.
Eric Teague singing down in Napoli
About the oak, the ash and the rowan tree.
Imagine too, Robbo, Ron and Chilly Blake
Drinking from a Spanish cider lake.
And an influx of European quota squatters,
In place of Broad Campden's farming Potters.

Horse drawn carts ploughs and binders
Sit in open air museums - sad reminders
Of an age that seems to be slipping fast,
Or has already - gone beyond the past.
Now! it seems, one must have a top degree
Before let loose to plant a bean or pea.
So - to those who want to close the changing gate
I fear you are at least a generation late!

Green Cries Under Violet Skies

I stop - proceed but mostly linger
Under violet skies - appearing blue
Their proper hue
Finding it hard to break through
To eyes not seeing sky's colour true.

Then walk on - with age attached – on Haines' hill
And fill my lungs with her fresh air
And do not spare her, her deserving due
Enraptured in such ceaseless wonder,
Captured in her 'plural compass pointed' view.

Looking forward over mounds of scarifying lime
My mind takes me through portals stretching far through time
To find that familiar escarpment rises
Have given sway – fallen away from custom
To be arrayed with a spread of omnipotent surprises.

I sweat with the heat under global warming's cowl
Spread over treeless orchards -
Ploughed and harrowed in by disc and scuffled now
To a rocky outcrop - prepared I'll vow,
For future terraced lines of dark fruiting vines.

Onward more, I see dense clouds of flies -
Drawn by desert heat to foul and dying meat
They seem shaken down like milled black peppercorns -
As though a prequel to the drenching
Of the untangled bramble formed by a dusty dry storm.

As the heat intensifies cross these northern skies
Those contours of thornless brambles
Now ramble - hung with dotted lanterns lit with fruit,
Soon to luminesce in lime or navy blue -
Demanding attention - commanding the view.

Back my daydream shudders now
Shocked into a thankful present - sprayed green
With sprouts, full knotted for the knobbler's chore,
To pick them by the score.
All weighted – all paid - the picking's made
But for how much longer – how much more?

Garden Dressing

Burnished coat of crumbling leaves
Formed as a ragged cloth
Cloaks the winter garden
With a decomposing broth
Of laburnum's poison dross
Caught on a fall of willow girth
To spread a cope of mould
Over winter's dormant earth.

Nature's mulch of droppings
Take up their cold repose
While the mighty hornbeam's bark
Is shred - to mulch the hard pruned rose,
Sought by a rest of starlings
Who spit out a fractious squawk
When caught out - by the silence
Of - a swooping Sparrow-Hawk.

Cold sits the pre-dawn air
Not yet loosely warmed
By December's brittle orange bowl
As yet without her light or shadows formed.
Still the cold is bruising on the mouth
Causing nostril hairs to shake
As vibrato epiglottis chokes
And fresh filled - shrinking molars quake.

A vole has just passed on-
Near to the creaking orchard gate
Decomposed by now
To a reeking sour bait.
While the earthworm has hard tilled
To aerate afresh the autumn loam
And allow a leeching mix of compost
Through - to his under soil home.

Quiet now - is the message sent
From the dormant mole,
All those stiffened vagrant pests
And the sole remaining vole.
The fork has stopped her turning
And the trowel leaves well alone
For the snow has come at last
To spread - a dressing of her own.

Snow Down

Sleeping the night in silent spread
Deep in dreams of winter dread.
'Till woken by a strange daylight
Reflected from the snow - lay white.
It lights the slowly waking room
Like shafted beams from frosty moon.
This magic winter wonder land
Lasts till touched by human hand.

The snow around the wash house door
Is tramped upon the kitchen floor.
Melting, running water spread
Fallen from an old boot tread.
Patterns distorted - free to form
Coral islands somewhere warm
Or field resplendent in a barley crop
Till scythed away by dampened mop.

Outside the snow's no longer neat
Like starched linen clean bed sheet
Nor even in the least
Like surplice on the parish priest.
Now resembling a frothing brew
Shapeless – stained - no longer new
Rusting flakes look uninviting - cold
Like ferrous scrap waiting to be sold.

The ever shortening winter day
Too quickly is forced to pass away
From melting – slipping - slushy sound
To crunching frost upon the ground.
An arctic cloak of purple black
Brings a chill across our back
Takes control of walking feet
And brings from them a slipping beat.

Down hard the frost is gripping strong
Intent in tightly holding on.
Then while we sleep a new surprise
More snow falls with degrees of rise.
Brightly laundered is the snow display
Covering the once grey slush decay.
Now round men grow from virgin snow
To last till turned to water flow.

Late Sky

The late sky turned
From blue to purple grey
And let the coming black
Take over from the day
To close the dark faced shutter
On the harshness of her light
And opens up the magic door
To the treasures of the night.

The quiet of the evening
And the welcome peace she brings
Soothes our chatter battered ears
Clears deadened sound to hollow rings
With only a low disturbance
To announce the mole is out
In a swift nocturnal shuffle
That precedes a frantic rout.

Thus late evening called
The vermin out to play-
To dance until a back was turned
Upon the homely dray
Where the badger sow would utter
Contempt for a fox that might
Decide to go to war with her -
In a kamikaze fight.

Lush broad leaves let chlorophyll
Absorb those deadly vapour spores
And refine them into oxygen
To be released from her green pores -
Back into the cautious ozone
As a life enhancing gas so pure -
To fill a trillion empty aureoles
With replenished air once more.

Dung beetles roll all other's drops
Discarded over time,
While avoiding hungry players
Caught up in nocturnal pantomime -
All moistened as they are
And refreshed by after sunset dew
Each views the others as a danger
Or - the perfect sunset stew.

The owl calls out 'I'm King
When in my silent flight-
With my ripping claws and beak
And my perfect midnight sight
I will take a mouse or beetle
Sad vole or dashing shrew
Full grown worms and baby rats
And a bleating chick or two'.

But weather snake or toad
Small mouse or insect pest
All must succumb to rising dawn
And give the daylight best.
For the sun lights up the Earth
With her scorching light
And closes fast - the magic door
Upon the treasures of the night.

Quiet Water Brook

Over quiet water, brook,
Was built a sleeper span.
To carry crop filled truck
And common labouring man.
Where the quiet water's yield,
A brighter view, and sweeter smell,
Winding over cowslip fields,
As clear as any drinking well.

Beneath the quiet water brook
The stickleback is seen to bite
Upon the tadpole - legless took
And downed in losing fight.
The Moorhen flies in hunger search
With plunging, underwater dive
Bringing fish up to her perch
To swallow down alive.

In the quiet water brook
The legs of boys do make
A watery trek to take a look
For an ancient, pirate lake.
The water soon is deeper
Rising way above the half
Of youthful striding shins
Squeezing boot to wading calf.

Upon the quiet water brook
Float twigs and leaves and straw.
And feathers from an eider duck
Who's nest was ragged once more.
Flotsam and jetsam floats
From people without names
Overtaking paper boats
Made for water racing games.

Runs the quiet water brook
From the pool of Haydon's mill
Where she twists around the crook
To wend her way at will.
She passes Jimmy Strange's -
On through the Loveridge ground
And across to Paxford ranges
Where she flows with bare a sound.

Cottage Remains

Striding quickly, slightly late
Through the freshly painted gate
Between the roses and the flocks
To the door set firm in hollyhocks.
Drawing breath I lift the latch
Of the door left on the catch
Opened wide I become aware
On calling out, there's no-one there.

An oak hat stand is in the hall
Pleasant scenes hang on the wall
Georgian sticks of polished brass
Reflect the open window glass.
The fire grate is cool and clean
Coated in a black lead sheen.
As I call out (with cough) once more
On passing through the kitchen door.

On the flags an old spaniel snores
By highly polished chest of drawers.
Willow pattern plates are stacked
Neatly on the wall in wooden racks.
Windows held on casement stay
Let in the sunny warmth of day
And an apron hangs upon a nail
Driven into the pantry door top rail.

Into the garden - onto the lawn
Where many years past Gran was born.
I step in search of signs of life
But see only trug and pruning knife.
Beneath the apple set in fine display
To greet the merry month of May
With buds of salmon pink and cream
Framed in a 'fruit leaf' summer green.

The silence only broken by
The bumble bee and hover fly
As my thoughts and ill bewares
Take me in and up the stairs.
Slowly, with finger tips, I push
The bedroom door - I can not rush
My fears realised - my tear stains
Lie on my passing Gran's remains.

The Allotment Shed

The rain beats down
Her south west greeting
On an old allotment shed
Of leaking planks and sheeting.
The shed where rake
And shovel had been kept -
Beside a pile of sacks
Where an injured cat had slept.

Two drab clay pipes
Both cracked and chipped -
Are still there - propped -
Though one has slipped
From their abandonment
On the mouldy window ledge -
More vivid green by now
Than the wild-apple peppered hedge.

The clouds lift slightly
To bring a short relief
To the rusty leeching roof
And lost bounty held beneath.
A peck or two of onion sets
Spread out to dry for seed -
Above some aging tins of spam
Once stored as stray cat feed.

A plank long since missing
Leaves a natural vent -
While several more are creaking -
To form walls of discontent.
A pickle jar filled up with peas
Finds cause to roll outside -
Through a door once closed
But now blown open wide.

An old pair of unkempt boots
Long cast aside - with laces gone,
Rest now from calloused tenants
Who have long since travelled on.
Many months before preparing
For a swathe of garden seeds
Abandoned - now self cultivating -
Among a fine display of weeds.

The Fox's Rules

Reynard - be brisk to forage
At domestic poultry's door
Only take that which you need
But never stay for more.

For the red fox must beguile
And dispatch his prey before
He becomes the blasted quarry -
Blown to a bloody gore.

So dash through groves of thistle
Thorn thicket – black bushes - or
Be trapped by what awaits you
Before death's revolving door.

Cream And Ashen Gruel

Moonlight fell across the night
To splash the calm glazed lake
With an ever weakening stream
Of watered yellow spite,
Seen by the waiting tramp
As spittle from a serpent's tongue
Mixed with devil's cream -
Though not to light his traveller's dream.

A tramp of raw dishevelled hue
Weather beaten - lean of girth -
As though some time had passed
Since he'd last eaten.
His low guttural murmuring
Could be thought a short request –
Perhaps a plea
From a man long past his best -
For scraps - comfort - and a fair night's rest.

As he stood and shivered, I shivered too -
A shudder of recognition seemed to entwine
Itself around my frosted spine
As though drawn by some attraction
Seeking warmth or welcome
Or - at least in part a softening heart -
Or other 'like' reaction.

But he was caught – this tramp
A lurking poacher
With his limping purple lurcher
Both brought out to front of withy tree,
Dog giving out a saddening snort -
Now less keen -
Man appearing more lean - even
Than his coal-dust shadow had a right to be.

I looked once at this ghoul
About to be condemned to ashen gruel
But would not look the more
For I'd lost sore time – thus engaged -
Become enraged
By many of his icy brew
And wished not to feel that chill anew
Brought by this winter ghost
For I'd felt just such a chill so many times before.

The Bleating Market

The market square
Offers only pens of air
Where once
Stock was framed in care -
In those days
When the Wednesday fair
Prospered there.

The bleating now
Comes not
From a barren cow
Or weaning sow
But a car alarm
Bawling out
A God-forsaken row.

The Market hall's
Roof is still there –
Proofed to stem the maul
Of rain and sleet
And blizzard fall -
Sitting, peaked,
Over arch and pillar walls.

Gaunt – lean - pale
Eternal sleeping boys
Wail for the memory
Of a ghostly sheep pen rail -
Each dream hung
Rusting on a nail
Oxidized by hail
Shed from a bygone gale.

Now litter blows without care
Like tumbleweed across
The ancient square -
To spread its share
Of despoilment there -
Leaving me to despair -
Knowing no-one's prepared
To ever hold again
A (bleating) fat-stock fair.

Snowdrops

White bobbing heads
Adrift upon a lake of snow -
Those quiet nodding drops
Are first each year to show
With their willingness to crop
From under zero they dare to rise
Above winter's frosty sheet
To show all a spring-like guise.

White porcelain heads -
Thimble-like – are moving to implore
The scatty hen – 'take care' -
In a nodding semaphore
And to over winter bulbs
This silent message bring -
'Burst out from barren earth
To swell the birth of spring'.

Cream Daffodils

Daffodils bring in the spring
As blooming golden swells
Parading on their long green stilts
To dance - in their golden bonnets
Drawn up tight to show
That they are perfect for the spring -
Bound in emerald petticoats and frills -
Ringing as a message of bells
To herald the coming of cream daffodils.

Pink Roses

Her seductive bud
Came in – full round and pink
A pinker centre yet,
Bursting from drab winter's coat
To brew her nectar
In the summer's sun.
Her scent has bade him in -
To her and to her twin.
He could not resist
Such seduction in a floral bed,
Where breeze on nakedness
Brings them all to shiver -
While a fallen vestige does expose
A joy - delivered
In the form of an English rose.

Wait And Watch

Warm float dawn's distressed clouds
To gently change and then madly re-arrange
Their enigmatic message
Rain - shine - overcast
Will the summer come at last
Or - wait and watch
For omens to portend
That the coming season prospers -
Or is her long panting breath
Born to choke – to a suffocating end.

They who walk slowly and so broadly spread
Are wide too much and look to keep in touch
With plunging heads
Direct- onward- steadfast
In common they will not be last
To wait and watch
For their prayers to crops
That might prosper with the coming season
Or could all too soon wither -
Exposed - on parched and stone soil tops.

Rain- steady and in proper time falling
As a morning spray to damp the searing day
Will- as refreshment
Quench- lubricate- repast
Just enough to help us at last
To wait and watch
Lengthening day light hours
Cooled in the leafy months of accelerating green
Or distressed with aphid's multi-coloured fly
Ravaging latticed leaves between the showers.

They who will be shortly formed into a harvest corps
Know it is their earnest call to be reaping all
As with bent backs
Reap-winnow- cast
Till the final sheaf is tossed at last
Now wait and watch
For true drying of the maize
Beans and corn must all over winter well
And next years seed survive
Beyond the deathly chill of a winter's gaze.

These Times

These times of global warming
With their swell in hurricane storming -
Times for the changing of maps –
Reflecting the effect of melting ice caps.
An ozone layer that's worn too thin
To stop the sun's rays burning skin.
Times with no workable solution
To the build up of carbon pollution.

Times when political promises un-kept
Are defended as merely unsound – never inept
At variance with the truth - but never lies
And questioning them is no longer wise.
The constant fear of dumb litigation
The onset of media induced vegetation -
Times when we must be politically correct -
Even at the cost of basic respect.

Times when a damaged cannabis smoker
Is reduced to playing televised poker
Too depressed – he confessed
For sleep - or even for taking a rest.
And his night-mares - he feels
Are never-the-less real
Causing an apoplectic panic attack
About a future now inescapably black.

These times of telephone bugging
Drug induced - old lady mugging -
Savage attacks ruining slumbers
Recorded only - as crime incident numbers.
These times when the incision
Of more reality television
Has created a cult of celebrity
Taking the place of (once valued) integrity.

These times of machine driven minds
Self-interest seekers of more and more kinds
Eating micro-waved pap without any taste
Deep in their (password) own personal space -
Narcissisticly sealed in their gas guzzling cars
Equipped to take them to Ascot, Cornwall or Mars
Disgorging un-sustainable volumes of waste
Replete in cholesterol and a complete lack of taste.

These times of e-coli manning our hospital beds
Invading sick and elderly heads -
Sent home at week-ends barely alive
By a contract doctor who goes home at five.
So abandoned - old soldiers and spouses
Are left to lie with (young) war dead in funeral houses -
While the voice of progress markets the claim
That today's self-obsessed culture is in no way to blame.

Changing Light

The late afternoon sun
Shone through a private window
To form a dappled pattern
On a mottled kitchen wall
To fall - in geometric patterns
Onto a pinewood floor -
Run through an open door
And out into the hall.

To form a sharp mosaic of light
With dark - untruthful shade
Which laid a ghoulish pattern
Of harlequins and fools
Over tools - put out for use
On boards for pastry making -
Pans and trays for baking
And a set of culinary mules.

Such was the afternoon delight
Of low oranges and browns -
Till a thicket of over growing clouds
Blew across the warming day -
To lay a grimy blanket -
Thrown - like early night
Over salmon pink and amber light -
To leave the day a chilling grey.

Now low - in dungeon light
Life scurries for bedding leaf
Hard backed crusty beetles
Soft charcoal mice and rats -
Cats out on the prowl
To catch the careless mole -
Errant chick and witless vole -
Seen only by a silent flight of bats.

Till moonlight rolled aside the black
To end the spiteful storm
With the weakest window light
Of ashen yellow shafts - that fell -
Swelled by fanned out mullions
Onto the unseen wall
Abandoned till this colour fall
Birthed the unborn morning swell.

The Drover

The drover's job is by definition,
One that travels very slow,
Driving stubborn beasts the way
They have no wish to go.
And so it was for Jimmy Dunnit
Who left Longborough travelling east,
Walking over Bourton Hill
To collect some Batsford beasts.

While driving them through Blockley
It was clear time was very short.
He could tell by the church bell toll
And the clock upon the Court.
As he moved them down from Norcombe
There was no way that he could know,
That the squire had shot a Postman -
Caused by aiming slightly low.

The doctor prescribed for the postman
A two pound jar of iodine.
And then he thought for the Squire,
Perhaps a good red wine.
The wine to be taken in by mouth
To help bring peace of mind.
And the iodine rubbed on liberally
To the postman's raw behind.

The smell of good fresh blood
Had made the Foxhounds bark,
Which echoed right through Blockley
As far as Northwick park.
A yearling jumped the paddock rail
Landing on the eggs of a sitting hen.
The hen then flew into a vixen,
And was quickly taken to the fox's den.

Young Dunnit felt it was the time
For quickly moving on,
As he had had the blame before,
For not being in the wrong.
Off towards Broad Campden,
As the weather clouded over dull.
But things would warm up quickly
'cus Jimmy had lost a Fresian bull.

He reached the top of Brier Hill
When he became aware of the grim escape.
And knew he had to find that bull, before
He was accused of bovine rape.
He searched the highways and byways
For mile upon ever more wearying mile,
Until he chanced upon the bull,
Near a cow - with a very contented smile.

He had to move out fast
And hope they'd not been seen.
But poor Jimmy's other beasts
Had took to grazin' on the green.
What's worse they had eaten apples
And some raspberries from a punnet,
So they ran, with the gardening man
Shouting, " 'twas that Jimmy Dunnit."

Journey's end and the farmer said
"I'll pay you two and six".
Jimmy thanked him very much
But said, "I think I'm in a fix".
The farmer said "the job is done
So now you're on your own.
My advise to you, is to get it over with
By bein' on your way strait home".

His father took off his leather belt
And orders Jimmy's trousers down.
Then just as the thrapin' was over with
His mother took his half a crown.
Then sent him to bed without his supper,
So Jimmy has made a new rule.
He will never! play truant again
'cus he's better off at school.

The Old Black Crow

We was packin' up just ater fower
Late a'ternun and darkness was near.
It alus seems to 'appen the same
At that time of the year.
We wuz all froze, 'sept ol Bill Grove
He reckoned he wasn't cold no more,
Somethin to do with 'is sailin'
Up by Russia in the fust world war.

Some birds was settlin' in for the night
They was a perchin' up on the roof.
Bert Bruce chuckled as he though
He could play a bit of a spoof.
"What colour's that black crow"
Shouted Bert to Pecker Howell.
"I'm to busy to look",
Said Pecker, "a claynin' this trowel"

40

I asked ol' Pecker,
Who I always called Fred,
If 'e'd clearly 'eard
What Bert 'ad just said.
Pecker looked back and grunted
I'm too busy a claynin' these tools
To spare any of my time
A listnin' to fools.

We was back at it
Next day - just after eight.
Fust we lit a few sticks
In the Vicar's new grate,
'Cos the weather was worse
An' them birds had all flown,
So we urched round the fire
Listenin' to Bert 'avin a moan.

Fred's bike had fell over
An' his flask had just bust.
He Said "I've got nuthin to yut
Not even yesterd'y's crust",
"An' them birds 'ave all gone
So now I'll never know,
What was the colour
Of that ol' black crow".

The Huntsman's Cry

The huntsman's milk's run dry
'The fox is king', supporters cry
How will we sate our lust for blood
That we claim is for the country's good.
What now to lift the gloom
Of a winter week-day afternoon
Without the saddled stirrup cup
Of scarlet claret - hot to sup.

How to replace the thrill
That came to climax with the kill.
How barren will the gallops be
Without the madness goading me -
To chase the screaming horn
Through hedge of dormant thorn -
Across scuffled fields planted well
Or over upland - moor and fell?

Reynard can never rule as king
Unless we're chasing after him
To keep him sharp - to hold him keen -
And work the myth that he's obscene.
Oh God! Life's milk's run dry
Giving me a cause to cry
"How will I stem this flood -
Of lust for fox's blood?"

Cool Is The Reaping

A muddled moon gives way
To an indifference of pastiche
By height of day -

Faint shadows only, endorse the paint
On soft grass – hard hills – distant
In travel and dark in contrast
To the cultured green of planted hope -
Put in with crop.

A huddle of dishevelled roofs -
Spreading wild thatch – some dispatched -
Top the crumbling homes.

With vented pitch of rafters –
Or of grafter's – (hidden - clearing ditch)
Grumblings - coming
With a gruff and ghostly rumbling sound
Thrown by low day - and darkened underground.

Dogs scratch, beneath carts
Off work - in need of parts – (closed in barn)
Obscuring herb and salad patch.

Rotund containers wait (behind the solid gate)
For a half belly of grain -
Or full – if bulged by courtesy
Of filling sun shed rays
Unfouled by hollow squalls of rain.

Blushing globes punctured by black ringed wasps -
Polished seed boxes, foxed
By early fruit grub probes.

So - peasants must tend plantings - (often unseen)
For if moribund and misconceived,
Untended crops
Would let seeds drop - unsheaved
Grain let fall – to cloak as serendipitous blown weeds.

Happiness

Happiness can be found in a song well sung -
In a sporting achievement contested and won -
Playing one's part in a production well done,
More enjoyable still while one's relatively young,
As is climbing over stiles and ascending tall trees
Buzzing around with the wasps and wild honey bees.
Pretending to fly can be such incredible fun
Though - slightly subduing if one happens to be stung.

Happiness to some is a day long romp -
Or even stiffer north-country yomp
By lake – over hill – or through amber dale
While following a 'Wainwright' Lake District Trail.
But on such a walk one should be ready for a fuss
Because harm could well befall the majority of us.
We may be soused by snowfalls or hammered by hail -
Or even worse - get lost somewhere in Wales.

Happiness can though, be found in bold
Excursions designed to please both young and old -
Brisk walking – earnest talking – all, while
Loping over many a blistering mile -
To dine on char grills, something I thoroughly endorse
With any Barbecue being alfresco of course -
Though gnawing on charred ribs is not exactly sedate –
So I insist on eating mine with a fork, from a clean china plate.

Happiness can come in one's prime, so to speak
Best during those years just before one reaches one's peak.
It can flash with the dash of a girl in short skirt,
Stiletto heels - and a hurry on her way to work.
Simple pleasures that can be had over long hours
In meadows - filled with wild girls and prim yellow flowers -
Though perhaps wild and prim should at least be transposed
Not that I mind the way the sixth line is composed.

Happiness can be written in grey layers of dust
Or found in the tasting of pies with thick pastry crust.
It can be given or taken but never mistaken
For toast - when the choice is with fresh eggs and bacon.
It's sometimes a mystery we try to unravel -
Or found in the joys of long distance travel -
Though more recently I've preferred not to tempt fate -
Choosing instead, early nights – over staying out late.

Before Capture

We waved – we wished –
We wandered in the hollow mist
Of a silvered sapling morning
Whetted with a dry frost warning –
Throwing our voices with small concern
Against echo's sure return -
While drawn to tangle our unbound play
Against the spiders beware display.

Pure pantomime set in a time
Of sibling play and distant crime -
Of innocence without care or cause to roam
More than a supper's distance slip from home -
To fish for spotted gold newts, dotted green frogs
And harmless snakes desperate for a hide of fallen logs
Or salt-washed stones
Under which to rest their elastic bones.

How the sweet grass has soured now -
Black soil turned from rich beneath the plough
Where chasing crows once plucked grubs
From the tongues of untrained cubs
Throwing their still thin screeches
Out, to fall before full height or reach
Could justly bandy grief
To each perching - lurching - wormy thief .

A time beneath drab slates of roofing cloud
Where we charged each particle of gain aloud
To slip across the rolling ground
As if in a pleasure, forever bound
In dilatory ponderings –
Dressed to suit our (free of ration) wanderings
Towards adventures dusted down of fear -
Born in the shade of a bright idea.

A splay of self-playing piano keys
Bouncing rhythmically to avoid a stray with fleas
Before capture turned our white keys black
And bent - into a rib and furrowed back.
Bankrupt now are we once braves of pebble dash -
Authors of heroic deeds and gravel rash -
A willing - under shilling few that largess forgot
While lost in the pay of joy and tommy rot.

The Orchard's Milk

Below a hedgerowed mesh of cropless fields -
In Granddad's orchard lay – a fall of rotting apples
Brittled over grass - dry as last year's hay.
Grass that cursed the treading foot that crunched
Her unkempt nap - to crush the glistening path -
From dragging gate to snow-headed thorny bush.

The chill air - now splintered by an urgent mistle-thrush
Whose lack of tuneful voice seems to bring him a need to say
'Such sating of fallen apples was not my wisest choice
For my legs would not feel so numb – nor swollen bowel
Feel in such a mess if those splitting, reeking apples
Had been forked into their barrows and taken to the press.'

Each fruit, born from a ruff of snowdrop white
Wound round a rhubarb tinted head – first a puny spore -
Quick to mature - to a swollen globe of polished red
Fed by summer's sun and rain, until October brings her down -
Blown perhaps by early winter squall – or simply relinquished
Through an autumn lapse - as bait for nature's insect traps.

Once released from their sapless jangling tethers-
Apples fall - slowed by the ground – they are in their glory
Decomposing slowly - not rotting - till squirrel found,
Scarried, scarred and bruised by the long toothed rake
Grappling with her windfalls - lay with grass and thorn
Soon winnowed - to leave a crush of golden-yellow balls.

Turned down by winding jack the stressed and creaking press
Squeezes from her lap the first pot that flushes more
Of this delightful deluge of pure - keen amber sap.
Now poured - juice runs from flask to waiting mothered cask
Now squeezed as green as Irish silk - nectar brought by fermentation
To a honeyed tope – as sweet as any mother's milk.

Leaving The Field

So - has the huntsman simply been out-foxed?
Now Parliamentary law so keenly disapproves -
Those coursing dogs are held - sacked and boxed
As are the chasing ring of horses hooves.

Now parliamentary law so keenly disapproves -
Banned are those flailing scarlet coats
As are the chasing ring of horses hooves -
No more following a pack of baying throats.

Banned are those flailing scarlet coats
With the shrillness of their horns brought still
No more following a pack of baying throats -
Gone quiet from Meon across to Dover's Hill.

With the shrillness of their horns brought still
I will lie at ease under oak's fallen griddle bark
Gone quiet from Meon across to Dover's Hill
Though morning shows that death came under dark.

I will lie at ease under oak's fallen griddle bark
Without the threat of a bloody ritual execution
Though morning shows that death came under dark -
An eerie end – by trap or poison contribution.

Without the threat of a bloody ritual execution
An unearthly quietness - I sense has fallen on
An eerie end - by trap or poison contribution
From about the countryside I've known so long.

An unearthly quietness - I sense has fallen on
Those coursing dogs held sacked and boxed
From about the countryside I've known so long -
So - has the huntsman simply been out-foxed?

Overrun By Time

As if to time, it came overcast -
Though not with clouds of rain
More with clouds of loss -
Restrained - as if for her
As she leaves us here,
Gaunt with hollowed pain.

Timed are quiet clouds' whispers
To turn to a churning, boiling grey
As if pulsing to remind me
Of the things that I should do -
Formalities I must attend to
Prior to succumbing to my dismay.

Time now to react – inform –
Details to be relayed
An appointment with the registrar,
Tea with the undertaker,
Notice to put in the local paper
And family visits still to be made.

Over time cloyed devils clog my brain
Pour out their liquid mischief -
To wither rude clout - hither stewed doubt -
Boiling up emotional jar
To bubbling black - raging tar
Spilling - scalding over frosted belief.

Time for remorse cried - tears dried
On handkerchiefs noisily played.
Dark coats worn - oaths sworn -
The lowering - the last rites read
While responses wait to be said -
Wreaths to be laid – excuses made.

So time has us all designed to slow -
Sour - as is bitter sweet the summer rain
Brown - as becomes the virgin snow –
Heralded – but soon forlorn
Are we - the pale newborn -
In pubescence, youthfully frantic –
Or in aging – more pedantic -

As we are – in time - designed to slow -
So Indeed are we - pre-timed to go.

Pale Darkness

A low lit moon hung – washed out -
As though barely touched by brush of water paint
Her pale complexion shone weakly -
Falling, as though in a cream translucent faint.

An underplay of hedgerow sticks
Danced away their icy – icing-sugar hats of chilling dust
In a persistent – wind assisted motion
Blown in from Russia – (as if sent) to stir their turgid fust.
Darkened navy willow beacons
Sent their fans of unpollarded – moon-chalked veins -
Not daubed by almond leaves –
Towards a sky of cruel bruised grey, relentless rains.

Silvered liquid sapphires fell
Against a backdrop, streaked in coal and old white gold
Now that unseen shades of blue
Had turned black ice salt green and warm as liquid cold.

Rabbits puffed their charcoal coats
In a strange, almost primordial, ritualistic gesture
Of damp, dull dun defiance,
From the shelter of their warming brindled cluster.

As dawn rays came they plucked
Away the dark – her compassionless shades of black and white -
Replaced with faintest yellows and pinks -
And reds and oranges all spilling out to swill away the slinking night.

Harvest Parade

The drying corn is on parade
Each greying head of straw
Was grown - like swaying infantry
Brought to readiness for war.
Stood among a band
Of waving poppy reds
 Blown in turn - to brush against
Full purpled thistle heads.

This high display of vibrant gold
Spreads from the partridge hide
To find the filling lambs at chase
On a verdant clover ride.
While stretching necks of raucous geese
Cough from the thermal heat -
As they soar upon the welcome lift
That lofts without wing beat.

Hot August high, unmarked skies
Free from water spats of rain
Ripen weighty heads to bring
A marvellous sea of grain.
With topmost ears of bullion
Pointing more towards the ground
Now over weighted- waiting now
To be harvest downed.

Golden patchwork mends the green
Of skyward shooting peas -
As though sown to fallow grazing land
By stitching fence and trees,
Just as the fledgling partridge dons
His feathered flying suit
Combed by brier's needle thorns -
Protecting her black fruit.

Wild bees labour long
To pack their combs with sugar wax
Soon taken by the thieving wasp -
From behind hard working backs.
Those yellow-banded parasites
Take their fight into the air
Batter airborne working bees
And leave their larders bare.

Each shoot salutes the others work
In their race to set ripe seed
Seeds that burst the waiting chest
And swell the winter's feed.
Though errant grain will loose
From cradle husk and drop
To grow again next year -
As a wild cereal crop.

The Cam At Juliana's Gateway

Dull ditch - in stagnation
Now I see you lie -
Save for the ripples
From an errant dragon-fly;
Too languid to be stirred
By the freshened breeze
Thwarted as it blows against
The yellowed willow trees.

Dull ditch of indolent,
Green, punctured slime -
Pock marked by browning reeds
Reduced to sticks of grime;
You lie putrefied
In high summer stench
For want of your return
To a useful water trench.

Dull ditch of humid atrophy
In need of a freshening stir
That will bring you back
To the way that you once were -
A teeming crystal waterway
Of my boyhood dream,
A chatter of life - borne along
As a shimmering - earnest stream.

Dull ditch your sight, your smell –
Your silent, moribund decay
Causes me to close my eyes
And see you as you were yesterday.
A yesterday of ripe breasted newts –
Horny toads and common frogs
Joined by claw and croak
To spawn - in wet leaf bogs.

So dull ditch – stir yourself
And chatter to the core.
Be lifted by the freshening rain
And overcome the turgid gore.
Let dragon flies - preening wings
Be seen - mirrored all the more
In the silvered sheets of boyhood
Where I tarried – all those years before.

Mixers And Larks

How happy would I have dreamt -
Perhaps at least in part
If music had been informed
It was to be my chosen art.
But I was not availed of choice
For art chooses – or not chooses us
Unseen – quietly at conception
Without even a modicum of fuss.

Thus music chose to pass me by
Her notes scattered about to confound
My dizzy prickling ear drums
With a low cacophony of sound -
From the slow thumping dumpers
And diesel-driven mixer bark -
Belching out her choking smoke
To drown the song of tit or lark.

Winds blew - hail stones flew
Clattering on a shed of corrugated tin -
A roofer's mate arriving late
Served only to add to the din.
Trowels scraped and then rang out
While the one-armed plumber cursed -
First at his dripping teenage mate
And then at the pipe that had burst.

The wheelbarrows incessant squeak
Was replaced with a groaning thud
Because it's wiry old pusher had tripped
And then fallen - face down in the mud.
He was completely ignored
As he slowly climbed to his feet
For the lunch-time hooter had blown
And the workforce had rushed off to eat.

As I sat down to my ten minute break
I began to wish that I had dreamt harder
For – well if not music then employment
Less noisy - to pay for the food in my larder
The boss meanwhile wore a broad smile
At the thought of the whole undertaking -
It's speed of advance and of course
At the thought - of all the money he's making.

Crow's Nest

Cock feather from a sparrow's tail
Bents of straw from broken bale -
A twist of coarse wool - torn
And tangled on a sharp blackthorn.
A lock of filched red cotton thread
Gleaned from open garden shed
Carried high to crown of larch
To rough a creche by end of March.
A place for warming mottled eggs
Held between parental legs
To incubate the coming brood -
Brought to life in sombre mood -
Incensed by a weaning brew
Cold as the arctic chill that blew
A chastity of frozen snow
Through which they had to grow -
As due reward for the frenzied glow
Of lust – from the cocky crow.

Crow's Rest

The starling dressed
Before the slumbering nest
Of highly polished spies -
Soon to rise
And out bleat the speckled thief
Whose breakfast brief
Was to 'Take them by surprise.'

Crow's Best

Spit out the earwig
A dried and choking crust
Disgorge the dehydrated slug
Rolled in limestone dust.
Eat only succulents
Sweet and easy to digest -
Like the jackdaw's cousin
A crow who only eats the best.

On The Farm

I was sent to do some helpin' out
The shepherd with a bottle o' stout
For 'e was in the lea a shearin'
With 'is brother, who was 'ard of 'earing.
I told him how a ewe 'ad strayed
Across some 'ay just freshly made
An' into the Parson's pasture
The same as she did last year.

His brother stared as 'e repaired
A puncture in the bike they shared,
Then 'e shouts, "What you need
Is one of these to gain more speed,
For you must go a gret deal faster
To stop the Parson gooin' past yer."
See - the brother 'ad broke 'is 'earin' aid
While courtin' with the milkin' maid.

Well! I 'ad just come from the farm
Where their dog 'ad met with 'arm.
In fact, it was in a serious state
Caused in a way I shall relate.
For I was there when 'is wife cried
'Cos their whippet pup 'ad died
A gnawin' on the telephone -
Which he'd mistook for an old 'am-bone.

I told this story to the brothers
Who in return related many others.
One about the giant mouse
Frightenin' a woman 'elpin' in the 'ouse.
Her ran out an' tripped full length,
Getting wedged in the garden fence,
An' bein' still stuck fast
When the tinker an' 'is donkey passed.

They did not tell me just 'ow 'e
Did set about to let 'er free
Nor what part upon that day
Did 'is donkey 'ave to play,
But they insist that if misused
The lady now is much improved.
Now employed in a travellin' fair,
But it's not clear what she does there.

Then the church clock struck ten past five;
Time for us to start to drive
Them ewes back up the 'ill, no doubt,
When we 'ears the Farmer shout,
"My wife's gone into early labour
So I've left 'er with a neighbour."
'E tells me to take 'er to Dr. Dare
So she can have professional care.

I puts 'er in the ol' Ford truck
Takin' care to first clean out the muck,
But that truck was gooin' awful slow
When she tells me she's about to go
An give birth like travellin' folk,
'cos she sez 'er water's broke.
So by the time I reaches the Doctor's place
He's greeted by a red an' wrinkled face.

The Docter sez "Now all's bin done,
We need to register your new son."
They turned an' asked me where
I thought was the start of 'er despair.
I told 'em the baby did start to come
Somewhere up on Westington
But the birth 'ad continued 'til
We was half-way down on Bourton 'ill.

They took out a certificate
Upon which they wrote the date
In the place of birth they 'ad t' say
Where the boy was born that day
So they made a decision that
They'd enter the following parishes at
Blockley, Batsford and part of Bourton
And just for luck they added Moreton.

I drove back to break the joy
To the farmer that 'is wife 'ad 'ad a boy
An' told 'im that the registration
Was complicated by the situation
Of us travellin' from place to place,
Which he said 'ad compromised his race,
'cos now 'e sez 'is new son, Stanley,
Be the only mongrel born into their family.

The Garden Prize

The bucket in which
He once had so much trust
Now lies in holes
Brought by age and crumbling rust.
A bucket once called on to water
Newly set and planted seeds
Is now beyond use
Even as a bin for pulled up weeds.

Chipped and broken terracotta
Spawl-sided earthen pots
Now only fit to hold
Last season's late shallots
And onion sets with flaking skin
Brought on by a winters sloth -
Or a few bulbs never planted
As this season's (intended) new growth.

The broken-down old potting shed
Stands as a greying scar -
Even her worm-riddled door
Is left dragging - partly ajar.
A long dagger of glass
That fell from a cracked sepia pane
Lets in a green holly bough
With last year's nesting robins again.

His two old War department
Copper watering kettles
Have long been lost among the brambles
And high grown stinging nettles.
Overgrown with them
Are a dozen carpet rails
And a lidless crock tea-pot
Turned home to a slime of inedible snails.

But undaunted is he as he dreams
That his garden's sad disarray
Could produce with moderate planning
A prize-winning allotment display.
His squeaking wheelbarrow
Has a flat tyre
And is of no use at all
For taking debris to the green smoking fire.

The water butt has filled with rain -
While a cover of leaves from the beech
Has formed a stale green liquid
Which is by now beginning to leech.
Oosing with a smell
Like that of a rutting tom cat
Though the stench is more likely
To have come from a decaying dog rat.

Enthusiastically he quickly bends -
Causing a shock to his arthritic back
Which buckles his knees
With another attack
Of restricting – stiff-jointed movement
To add to his painful rheumatics
Causing him to walk with unnatural gait
As a ham would in amateur dramatics.

The orchard compost box
Has been stuffed to over full -
The pruning saws do not cut
And the shears have come over dull.
The ash rail fence has blown down
Bringing a further two broken posts
And the whole place seems infested
With those crawling (after dark) ghosts.

So he stops for a while
On the bench for a rest
Beneath the mauved lilac -
(In view of a hedge sparrow's nest) -
Where he draws on his pipe
And sups from a large mug of beer.
Then smiles - as he closes his eyes
Knowing he can do all the weeding – 'next year.'

Conies

We went in search of conies,
Known as rabbits to most of you.
We sold their skins to the tanner
And ate their flesh in rabbit stew.
They saved the folk from hunger
Who lived in rural degradation
And fed the tramping classes
To prevent their night starvation.

We left them alone in breeding
So their numbers wouldn't dwindle.
Or, just tried to take a single buck
And leave the does in kindle.
If we found the young abandoned
We'd raise them for their meat.
But we always knew we wouldn't kill
Those we couldn't eat.

Most Sunday mornings early
With ferret box upon my back
We'd set off for the fields
Bounded by the railway track.
We'd cycle to the moors
Then set foot in muddy boots
To walk through fields of corn
And sometimes winter roots.

We would meet with Albert Potter
Near the Paxford ditch.
We would have the ferrets
And he'd bring his collie bitch.
The ferrets sent the conies out
The collie made them run
And Albert finished off the job
With a double-barrelled gun.

My Father had a butcher's bike
Which we would load the prizes in
Several pounds of good fresh meat
And two bob's worth of furry skin.
Out of their coats and in the pot
Such stew would make us gorge,
Thanks to our good cook Mother,
And rabbiting Father - George.

White Acres

How broad the snowy pasture lies
Beneath the single goose - that flies
Across ever darkened winter skies -
Drawn to rest by screeching cries.

How harsh December's blanket freeze
Falls - to swamp late swarming honey bees –
Or snap the fruit from hedgerow trees -
Bar ash – a chandelier of clustered keys.

Scant movement flits with scarce a bound
As though an echo to a hollow sound
Heard above – below and all around -
As a wassail sung on wintering ground.

Now my gnarled and calloused fingers wait
To push through snow fouled garden gate
And find my chair to sit - unmoved till late -
From hot, flaming, well logged grate.

With crackling red and yellow glow -
Hawthorn blocks put on a dancing show
For their flickering players to have me know
How fine life was - all those years ago.

Years when - still green enough to bend
And callow too - enough for mind to lend
Itself to high adventure – then a friend -
But now gone like me beyond a boyhood's end.

Haydon's Field

A field of reeds - of poplar trees -
                Of undulating sheep
Bent to graze beneath the haze -
                On Juliana's keep.
A keep of glee - of humming bees -
                Of green winged flies
Brushing their legs over osier beds
                To make the pollens rise.

A meadow of lime - of yellow celandine
                Of green and golden dog
Who ends his slide to chide a shy toad
                Hid beneath a fallen log.
A log of decay – of old squirrel dray -
                Of fat field cats
More than willing to take on the killing
                Of anti-social rats.

A surround of stones – of five bar gates
                Of beech and wire fence
Loosely thrown around from hedge to ground
                Where growth was not so dense.
A defence of need – Of rough hewn stakes -
                Of stone surrounded arch
Built astride the road that tried to halt
                The roundhead's march.

A place of springs – of garrulous stream -
                    Of one time corn-mill pond
Turned from winter ice to Easter spice
                    By spring's coming wand,
A wand of recall – of bygone dreams,
                    Of school day plays
And games performed by childhood names
                    During timeless holidays.

A graze of geese – of wild fowl leas -
                    Of spirits revealed
By mysterious fears that stayed for years
                    In this moribund field.
This field of reeds - of poplar trees
                    Of undulating sheep
Bent to graze beneath the haze –
                    On Juliana's keep.

Tractorin'

You should see the state
Of our five barred gate
Since Bert took the tractor
An' very quickly backed 'er
Right over a pile o' stakes -
Just one more of 'is mistakes -
Causin' 'im to lose control
An' bringin' down a 'lectric pole.

Well I knew things wus bad
When the Farmer 'e went mad
T'was the size of the bill
That 'ad made 'im so ill.
So off to hospital the gaffer went
Where ol' Bert 'ad first bin sent.
Farmer was a moanin', "I be done
For Bert, be layin' in next bed but one".

Well we all thought we should
Get on as best as we could
With some disc 'arrow 'oein'
An' then start the winter sowin'.
Till when we 'ad trouble with a disc
Which put the midwife at some risk
When it flew off from it's spike
Through the wheel of 'er delivery bike.

As best as I can recall
'Er's was not a graceful fall
So t'was with some embarrassment
We 'erd an ambulance 'ad bin sent,
While bein' relieved t'was not an 'erse
A bein' sent for the prostrate nurse.
I prayed they would not keep 'er in
Nor tell the boss - 'er next o' kin.

I 'ave to say the Farmers not too well
'E's a bein' kep' in a padded cell.
The nurse can no longer do 'er rounds
She's sill a 'earin' funny sounds.
I suggested she should take care o' 'im
After all 'e is 'er cousin, Jim
T'was then she struck me with 'er shoe
Shoutin' "I needs no advice from the likes of you".

Well me an' the foreman, Ticker
Went for some advice from off the Vicar,
Who did not 'ave much t' say
'Sept we should get 'em all to pray.
So we set off for the Plum an' Pear
As all would be a drinkin' there -
A toast to Meg who'd just got married
Or was it 'er dad 'ad just bin' buried?

Seein' the state we found 'em in
T'was no good a tryin' to stop their sin
So Ticker took the barmaid's arm,
And ordered with all 'is charm,
For 'im 'e'd 'ave a double gin
With ice an' a slice of lemon in
An' for me 'e said a bitter dash,
'cos was slightly strapped for cash.

The hours they just seemed to fly
As most of us was gettin' high
An' I feels there is no cause to doubt
The Gaffer's plight 'ad bin forgot about.
So it seems t'was as I 'ad feared
As Ticker an' the barmaid disappeared
For of the gaffer an' 'is despairs -
I've got the feelin' no-one cares.

Porridge

Adulterated oatmeal
Boiled and let go cold
On a bright blue gas ring
Of piped in natural flame -
Congealed now for ever
Not again to be the same -
Nor would the suffering boy -
Or so he would make claim.

He rose each day to frost
That chilled the draughty room
With his lament -
Or more a desperate prayer -
In which he claimed
His mother didn't care -
And would rue the day
When he was no longer there.

Nor could he grasp just how
His sister was allowed
To take her place at table
And then to calmly boast -
That because she was the one
Who had protested most
She would be the only one
Eating marmalade on toast.

So the bowl and spoon
Set at the breakfast place
Filled him with an oat malaise
That caused a chilling groan.
Though as he grew so well
It seemed a hollow moan -
While his mother's faith in porridge,
Had now been clearly shown.

Wood Street Corner

The shop on Wood Street Corner
Next to the haberdashers
Had sold for many years
Just sausage, pies and rashers
But now has gained a noteriety -
You couldn't call it fame
For supplying all and sundry
With course shot wild game.

The pheasant and the partridge,
The grouse and woodcock rare,
Plummet to the killing ground
To quiver – near a fresh shot hare.
Blown to death by week-end gun
With a double barrelled name
Displaying - with a crass guffaw -
His bag of fresh shot game.

Spoils of Rigor mortised feathers -
Fur - matted in congealed blood
Are tossed upon the tractor tail
And driven - from the wood,
To dangle till a fortnight hence
From the salt house curing frame
To reach the table after fish -
Stuffed - as well-hung game.

Tiers of speckled eggs
Serve time in automation
Un-caressed by parent claw
Through weeks of incubation,
Hatched to feed, de-beaked
By those who strive to claim
"We only did as we were told"
By raising next year's game.

Beaters and their howling dogs
Again cause wild birds to fly -
So that the waiting gun can blast
His quarry from the sky
And then berate a passer by,
Who claims his sport is tame,
Bellowing, "There is always risk
When hunting wild game".

Quiet Grief

She was born- she stayed a while
And then was called to leave.
In between she strived to smile-
Succeeded to a large degree
Through any cause to grieve.

Grief – unspoken - quiet.

Though others too are born - stay a while
Then find that they too
Are obliged to leave
On their mournful day -
While others stayed to grieve.

Grief - expressed in whispers.

She - being born stayed for her time
To strive - to bring a smile -
Work hard before she had to leave.
Though so in earnest to succeed
She hardly had the time to grieve.

Knowing grief – fades in time.

In time others of whom she grew fond
Will have to take their leave
Unsought - taken to their spirit life -
Each on their mournful day
While those left can only grieve.

Grief – hushed - no sound.

But she was not born forlorn
Though given cause to mourn
Before her time to leave -
Giving us her legacy of hope
Amid our cause to grieve.

We - in grief quietly bow –
And hold that hope closer now.

Epitaph

In life no hope -
In death just one -
That there could be
In someone's mind,
A thought for me.

The Merry Lark

Where has gone the Merry Lark
Who sang each morn across the park
Calling us all from horsehair bed
To greet the dawn and day ahead.
Oh how that cheery lark did speak,
With clear voice through open beak
Of the page that each day holds
Another tale yet to best unfold.

Where have gone thoughts, spread,
Shook like dust from wooden head,
To lay between the shrinking boards
There - held from their right accords
Till the low blown open door
Lets in a breeze to sweep the floor
And help float those dusty hoards
As though towards their just rewards.

Will they return to the empty park?
And find again the missing lark.
Will he be drawn to orchestrate,
With Robin Wren, an early date
To play with billowed open throat
The warbling of a simple note -
To tell again of joys each day will hold
And adventures yet to best unfold?

The pigeon's cooing can not compare
With the lark's fine morning air
He brings only noise and mess
And makes demands without finesse.
This grey feathered basking shark
Is the main despoiler of the park -
Not a guest we would like to stay
But instead a pest - we urge to fly away.

The day of bustle turns to rich delight
Under darkened cloak of middle night
The pigeon's gone and lark's asleep
While men with brushes come to sweep
The litter spread throughout the day
Into bins - to then be wheeled away -
So the dawn shows up a cleaner park
To welcome back the Morning Lark.

Settling Billy In

We was settlin' Billy in
A job we had to do.
For 'e 'ad been away
Ater 'e'd offended one er two.
'E cut up the Vicar's lawn
An' ripped 'is gardener's smock,
Ran in through the back door
An' broke the mantle clock.

The Vicar 'ad wrote a sermon
Entitled, "Future at last",
'Til Billy got a 'old of it -
Now the future's in the past.
'Is 'ousekeeper used the dustpan
To sweep the remnants up
An' tipped next Sund'y's sermon
Onto the midden yup.

The Reverend and the council
Of which there was a few,
Met in urgent session
To decide what they should do.
They would 'ave young Billy watched
Both through the night and every day,
Except for Christmas and the New Year
Which would cost 'em double pay.

It was not easy for the Verger
To take on the extra job
Of lookin' after Billy
With 'is other duties, all for fifteen bob.
'Is wife was forced to give an 'and
An' 'is daughter too.
So they kep' Billy company,
An' fed 'im on leek an' carrot stew.

They tried to keep an eye on 'im
An' stop 'im from causin' any woes.
Until one day 'e slipped away -
Well, that's 'ow the story goes.
At the village duck pond
Where 'e'd 'ad it on 'is toes,
'E butted Mrs Parsons through the hedge,
And then - Mrs Hedge's Parson's nose.

The village Bobby was called back
From 'is visit, to the Doctor's daughter,
To assist the local fire brigade
To pull they women from the water.
There was a gret fuss made
An' an enquiry instigated,
Which clearly couldn't prove
Weather, they women an' Billy was related.

The enquiry did recommend
That the pond should 'ave a fence
In order to prevent such crimes -
As acts, of water violence.
All parish stock should be secure
An' only sold by sealed bids.
An' an eye kept on those two ladies,
In case they should 'ave kids.

Parental Guidance

You don't need to see the news
You're too young for holding views.
So just you mind your P's and Q's,
And go and clean those filthy shoes.

You should be more like Kate,
You never ever see her late.
Don't lie in bed and vegetate,
Get down here and clean this grate.

You make sure you stay alert,
And put down that leather skirt.
We don't want another cousin Bert
All blue cravat and bright pink shirt.

I don't know who you think you are,
Demanding a ride in Fred's new car.
Will you put down that biscuit jar?
One day my lad, you'll go too far.

I knew your exams would be flop -
Now run me an errand to the corner shop.
Oh! And give that kindling a final chop,
Then give this kitchen floor a mop.

You spend too much time at ease,
Think that money grows on trees.
That you can do just as you please,
While I'm on my hands and knees.

It's hard raising a family on your own,
But it's not often you hear me moan.
I'm nothing like your Auntie Joan,
And leave that girl next door alone.

Well one day you'll be glad
That you listened to me, my lad.
I don't want you turning out as bad,
Nor going to prison - like your dad.

Snow Crow

Hobble – hop
Don't dare to stop
In frantic search
To fill the brood and crop.

Taloned claw
Must show talent more
To push home the bolt
On hunger's draughty door.

Scrape – scratch
Unearth a scrawny catch
To take
And feed a squawking batch.

Brush – blow
Ill fall of early summer snow
To find sparse fill
For un-feathered nestling crow.

Loud Crow

Blistered heaven
Sending down white puss
In a falling rage
It seems - to punish us.

Burying all beneath -
Upon which we sup
To starve us
Of our bowl and cup.

So we must wait
For sky's spleen to go -
Before we once again,
Can bleat and CROW!!

Proud Crow

Gnarled and wizen -
Toothless jaw
Does increase the need
For rest among fresh straw;
To seek a breakfast catch
On which to preen and glow
And show that pride
Lies deep - within the aging Crow.

Fifty Years Ago

I likes a laugh an I likes a drink
An' in the evenin' I likes to think,
Of Campden stun laid with mason's trowel
And Campden streets cleaned by ol' Jack Howell.
Ol' Jack was from the age of broom an' brush
When only bulls was in a rush
And farmers still showed their tegs
In streets with Gypsies selling pegs.

On the wireless we had Ned Larkin
An' roads with unrestricted parkin'.
Not as it mattered to the likes of us
Bein' Lucky to have a ride in 'Asum's bus.
We had bikes, mostly second hand,
To get us to work upon the land
Some Satd'ys we'd goo to Aysum, by steam,
To goo any farther 'ud a bin just a dream.

Our food was grown in garden rows,
Should've bin good for us - I s'pose.
The sort of grub today they calls organic
That stops the scurvy and the panic.
There was eggs straight from the hen,
If you could find 'em in the pen
And of course we was in the habit
Most Sund'ys - of a ferritin' for rabbits.

There was Reg Smith's wooden sheds,
'Is greenhouses and 'Is strawberry beds.
'E grew byuns and 'E grew pays,
Yes - them was 'good ol' days'.
We'd goo to work when the weather was fine
An' pick 'alf a pot for 1/9d.
You'd have to goo some for fourteen bob
What a blinkin' awful job.

We never went all that far,
Like them as did who had a car.
We'd stay and help Reg Howell to kill
The pig we'd raised on scraps and swill.
Porkers was raised for food and sellin' on,
Folks said they'd be glad to see 'em gone.
But as they went, you could see a sad look,
Even on the face, of Ol' Lawrence Ladbrook.

The Armistice Chair

Morning opens late this day
Subdued behind dense cloud -
Clad in an overall of flattish grey
Which granddad sees in quietly
From his Uncle Will's arm-chair -
Set there on Armistice Day.

He has learned to 'wear it well'
Like a coat cut to fit a corpse
Sat there - half dressed -
Entombed within the fading room
Where they will come -
And he will be assessed.

She will say, "You can not stand
Or dress yourself without a hand.
You do not wash from what I see
Nor make yourself a cup of tea.
So - you can no longer live alone -
It's time we put you in a home."

He will protest, "I have too much to do
To waste my precious time on you
There is housework to be done -
A dozen greyhounds need a run
And I must be here - well prepared
In case another war's declared."

But his protests will fall silently away -
Muffled by the growing dust
That chokes all lingering doubt
About his pleading fears
Soaked by then in his pathetic tears -
As they come to wheel the old man out.

Another life will end - before death
Takes pity on his panting soul -
Still in protest at being anywhere
Without those water-colour dogs -
A brace of twelve bore shotguns
And Uncle Will's old chair."

By the grave I 'm sure I'll hear Him say,
"I know they've had their way -
Covered me with ash and dust -
So I will go - if go I must
But I shall never! settle there -
So far from my Armistice chair."

The Benson Brothers
(Sunshine Plumbers)

It was a dreadful day
As I walked up through the Noel
Where I met two baggy plumbers
About one step from the dole.
The one I knows as Kevin
An' tuther, I think is 'is brother Ron –
Who was standin' there a moanin'
That 'e 'ad only one sock on.

So I sez, "This rain reminds me -
You boys said you'd fix me leaks;
An' that's more than a month ago
In fact I'd say nearer to five weeks.
"I'll tell you what," said Kevin,
"We'll come round straight away
An' if we don't you can be sure
We'll fit you in some other day."

Now I can trust young Kevin
For 'e is a dog possessin' man
Who owns at least one corgi -
'cause it's written on 'is van.
While 'is younger brother Ron
Is broad across the back
Good enough for 'eavy work -
Such as spud 'umpin' by the sack.

Well they arrived just a'ter five
An' left their boots out in the 'all –
Then went up to the bathroom
To check my plastic flush valve ball-
Which they set about an' fixed
With a washer in the box
For which I rewarded each of them
With a brand new pair of socks.

I said I was quite pleased -
As the sun - it 'ad come out again.
Where upon they claimed – "It's us
Who stopped the pourin' rain,
'cause we're the sunshine plumbers
Of much fame and great renown -
Well - at least from Aston road
Down to the Cricket ground."

Tom's Drum

They took their smoke with pills
And a shot of intravenous pleasure
To blow away the shark
And grasp the devil's measure.
They walked across the water
To join a Jamaican 'bacca group -
Drank a gill of happy juice
From a jug - of blue electric soup.

They sailed the sea for diamonds
Dressed in nothing but their beads -
Rolled up the dried out leaves
From an unknown crop of weeds,
Sent by a mystery cousin
Who lived somewhere overseas
In a package stamped Moroccan -
To help them shoot the breeze.

They lit their joints and swallowed
To let the tangled pain go-
And sailed into the cream lagoon
To find their spangled rainbow.
Where they saw the sea wash-out
A far off tidal moon
Reflected in the liquid spill
From a lightening white spittoon.

All of them now squatters
Caught in a dangerous bliss
Wrapped around the hazy queen-
Who seduced them with her kiss.
So now they dance until the last
Of the merry - gone insane -
Are washed away to purgatory
In a shower of raspberry rain.

Educating Ted

Dear Mrs Working Mother,
I feel obliged to write
To inform you of our
First year classroom plight.
The children attended lessons
And their progress thrived,
Until that is, the awful day
When your son Ted arrived.

He had one sock, half way up
And the other, half way down.
Then tripped upon his boot lace
And ripped Miss Teacher's gown.
Her glasses flew across the room
As she landed on her nose,
While her grasp, to gain composure,
Turned on the fire hose.

We accept, it may be fair to say,
That some problems are our fault,
But refuse responsibility for any damage
Done, by your son's catapult.
The glazier's here, three times a week,
Repairing a very large amount,
Of damage done by Ted, your son,
 So we must claim on his account.

Also! there is the matter of
The flood in the common room,
Caused by a four inch water valve,
Wedged open with a broom.
The head of which was later found,
Wrapped in an oily rag,
Attached to a three volt battery fuse,
In your son's homework bag.

Our Governors' sad decision,
To expel your son was made,
After a tough three hour meeting
And, help from the Fire Brigade.
They extricated the Ofsted man,
Who only then was able
To tell us we had finished bottom!!
Of the schools' performance table.

You may collect your son
At a time that suits your plan.
We've enclosed a map for you
To claim him when you can.
He's in an old asylum camp
At the place of indication.
It's emptier now - since Ted arrived,
Most inmates chose repatriation.

We notice from your application
That Ted has a twin brother
And we must say we're most dismayed -
That you expect us to take the other.
I must insist that you withdraw
This ill planned application
On the grounds of child welfare
And fear of further conflagration.

Though we do feel obliged to help
With finding them a placement -
If only to make much better use
Of the shelter in our basement.
We'll search as far as Timbuktu
Go far beyond the end of Wigan pier
So they may both be correctly schooled
In – well - anywhere but here.

Joy Or Happiness

Some years ago my Gran determined
To avail me of her philosophy on life.
"Make sure that all the kids are yours
But cast all doubt in favour of your wife.
Don't spend your hard earned money
On things you can ill afford -
Don't waste your time in seedy bars
Hand your life instead, up to the Lord."

"Spend more time inside the church
Kneeling down to pray -
Give a rousing call of thanks
When you hear the organ play."
But I could only think of the vicar
De-frocked for playing a game of sorts
With some sixth form choir girls
And the repercussions that it brought.

"Happiness isn't found," she said,
"On a long face stained with tears
It comes when you dry your eyes
And wash behind your ears.
You'll also find it when you're chopping wood
And cleaning out the fire grate
It also comes by sitting quietly
And finishing - whatever's on your plate."

"You'll always feel far better
If you have an early night
Because you will sleep more soundly
And wake up feeling nice 'n bright.
Happiness will come to you
When helping those worse off
And the time you spend out in the air
Will cure that sickly bar room cough."

"Gran - I've stood here while you've lectured -
I even listened once or twice
To your ever present wisdom
And well meaning good advice –
But I feel that I must remind you
That I'm now a grown up boy
Who would gladly give up happiness -
For a night in bed with Joy."

Deciphering A Flat Pack

A slightly grubby pantechnicon drove by
Then reversed - to darkening my door.
Shortly there-after my bell gave a ring
Then again - as though having a fit
And before I could reach it
The annoying device rang several times more.

Gasping breathlessly I answered the call
Where I saw a faded blue and white van
With a very large dent
Punctuating an address - somewhere in Kent
And a battered brown clip board
In the hand of an over rotund - shabby overalled man.

He didn't bother to look up as he chanted
I've brought some of your order -
So where do you want me to drop it off luv'
Then – finally when he did raise his eyes
He seemed somewhat surprised
As he muttered – 'err sorry - my mistake Guv."

Once we'd unloaded the packages listed as mine
He handed me a pen and rather damp docket
Which I was reluctant to sign
Until I'd thoroughly checked all the items were mine.
Finally I signed and handed the note back -
Though his pen seemed to fall in my pocket.

I opened the first pack and looked down inside
At the reams of instructions and was forced to conclude
That I was - in truth - totally confused -
The assembly procedure - though surely prolific
Seemed to be written in code hieroglyphics -
So I left them unread – somehow not wishing to intrude.

I struggled long with this pressing dilemma
Until finally I'd reached my limit -
At which point I rang my young nephew Alf
Who'd taken a gap year and was finding himself –
He said, 'though he was deep in his meditation -
For a tenner – he could be round in three or four minuets.'

Alf arrived promptly - soon setting to work -
Once of course – we had settled his generous fee -
He re-assured me that he would soon have the job done
It was just a matter of making logical deductions
From 'clearly' laid out - assembly instructions.
"After all" – He chirped, "How hard can flat-pack assembly be."

I told him how I'd been consumed by foreboding
As though I'd uncorked a bottle and took out a note
That when read had given me an unearthly chill –
Rather like sneaking a look at an unauthorized will –
Which brought from Alf this philosophical view -
"If things weren't meant to be read - they'd never be wrote."

"Please!" He continued, Forget about wills and outstanding bills -
What we both need is some good filling grub -
I've had not a bite since early last night
So forget all about bottled up messages
And concentrate more on egg - bacon and sausages."
His keen point of view left only one thing to do -
So we departed to re-assemble across at the pub.

Alf's Dilemma

The bottle's message became clear
Now drained quite empty of beer
Alf said - I'm sorry brother
Though it's time for another
They're refusing to serve us in here."

Alf's Humour

Being fond of a joke
Alf asked the bar bloke
If he could have one with Mick
Or even a couple on tick
Which caused the Landlord to choke

The Barman's Claim

If you're seeing spirits and such
And think that you're still in touch
Then my message to you gents
Is that it's time that you went
Cus you've already made contact too much.

The Landlord's Last Word

He said your stupid suggestion
Has given me indigestion
So yes it's far too late
For you to open a slate
And a 'lock-in' is out of the question

Electrifyin' Cup

Ol' Cup went t' the Lion
Where 'is uncle Charlie said,
"I 'ear's you'm on the 'lectric
In the 'ouse; an' the shed".
"Ah - it's amazin'", said Ol' Cup,
" 'ow well I now can see -
Since I bin electro-cuted
By the M.E.B."

"Though th'oil gives good light -
When it's a burnin' well
There's times it starts a smokin'
An' givin' off an awful smell.
But that 'lectric – so I'm told
Be the best of lightin' stuff -
Never givin' off black smoke
If not burnin' clean enough."

"Course I've got gas for cookin'
That's good there is no doubt
But it smell's summut awful -
When the wind 'ave blown it out.
An' if you'm not too careful
It do boil over - an' then spill,
So you finds yer bloomin' gas rings
Gets crusted by a pot o' tater swill."

"But 'alf a minute Cup."
Said the shillin' meter mon,
"Accordin' to my readin's
You've never switched it on."
"Well now," said Cup,
"That's not quite right,
'cause I 'ad t' use it once
T' see - t' get me lamp t' light."

The meter mon said, "Cup
It's not worth you avin' 'lectrc in."
For mostly when we calls
There's no money in the tin."
"Ah!" says Cup, " I 'ave complained
About you shillin' meter men
'Cause every time I puts a shillin' in
You comes an' takes it out again.

Charlie's Layers

Upon my paper round
One place I used to stop
Was at ol' Charlie Ladbrook's -
Behind his Butcher's shop.
Through the alley at the back
Was where I found ol' Charlie sat,
Eating tomatoes with pork pie,
While dropping crumbs on his ginger cat.

"Come in 'ere my bwoy,"
I'd 'ear old Charlie shout
"I be in the kitchen 'ere,
Though today I 'ave bin out.
I've 'ad to do some gardenin'
And mend me chicken pen
For every day this ruddy week
I've lost a layin' 'en."

Although I was feeling sorry
Charlie said "Now don't you worry lad
I've got another source of eggs
So things be not too bad".
'e showed me an ol' basket
Filled – 'e said to me -
With some of the ripest eggs
'e'd got from his 'layin' tree.

He said the eggs was secret
And 'id beneath the bottom leaves
Where 'e would often come across
A plate of bread and cheese.
He said he once found mouldy faggots
And two screw top jars of lard -
But lately things was not so good
Since Pyment's cleaned his yard.

Yesterday - Ernie Lockyer looked
From the window of the Mill -
Saying as 'ow 'e felt
That the chickens looked quite ill
And 'ow his worry was
That the chickens wouldn't lay.
But Charlie said, " don't worry lad-
They 'ave bin layin'- out in the sun all day!".

Blue Cart

Blue cart – rest –
Rest and then go on
To house the harvest
While now the sun is strong.
Take the ripened crop –
As still the summer warms
To the terra cotta shelter
Covered - to stave off the coming storms.

Blue cart - heave –
Heave hard the golden straw
On your knotted planks
Until there is no more
To urge the screeching axle
Through gnarled and creaking door,
To lay a sweeter bed
On the byre's dry earth floor.

Blue cart – un-nerve -
Un-nerve those mice and rats
Already put to flight
By a brown and orange cat
Who has too often been disturbed
By tiresome rodent bleats
That souse the sleepy afternoon
Already soaked in stifling heat.

Blue cart – give -
Give the donkey leave
To draw those iron tyres
Through the standing sheaves
And accept his angry snorts
As just a rude display -
Some might consider wholesome –
In their simple - rustic way.

Blue cart – inspire -
Inspire those who paint
To set you on a canvas
With brush of light restraint -
So those who have not seen
Can be brought to know
Of the timeless charm elsewhere
In parts – they might never go.

Yubberton Regis

As I crossed the Battle Bridge
I thought I 'erd a squawkin'
So I stopped an' saw it was
Two Campden Crones a talkin'
They 'ad 'erd that Yubberton,
With ower Mayor an' Corporation
'Ad a platform booked in May -
All day at Campden Station.

I approached they women,
Lizzie an' 'er sister Gert
With a certain sense o' caution
For I was a wearin' my best shirt
An' they was known as fightin' 'ens
Who couldn't take a joke
An 'arbourin' a poor attitude
Towards we Yubberton folk.

I tipped my cap in some respect
An' bid them each good day
They made clear by loud reply
They wished, for me to go away.
I took two quick steps back
An' then I did contend
That I wished to hear their story
Right to the very end.

Well! they calmed down enough
Through chewin' my tobaccer
To relate their sorry tale
Which was one of a sobbin' matter.
Campden Town 'ad bin turned down
An' so 'ad lost to us, the privilege
Of a visit from the Royal Prince,
Now 'anded over to ower village.

We set about to raise much needed funds
By a stall put up for bring an' buy
All loaded down with jams an' cakes
Run by the Village W.I.
There was also courtin' rides
On 'orse drawn loads o' hay,
Sadly they was quickly stopped
'Cause of the games some boys did play.
The Vicar formed a choir
For what we couldn't tell
'cus some o' they boys was taken ill
While the rest of 'em wasn't feelin' well.
The Parish council 'ad bin made
Into a Mayor an' corporation
So they could be much better able
To plan the comin' celebration.

Well we was all agreed
That those refreshments planned
Should be made by a usin'
Grub – only grown from ower own land.
An' then of course
We should 'ave t' roast a pig
Never 'avin' entertained before
A mon, not even 'alf so big.

The corporation coach was pulled by 'orses
With 'ighly polished brasses
An' then they was a waited on
By the finest of our lassies.
The mayor 'e was inside
A full of expectation
As the whole parade drew up
To stop, outside of Campden Station.

But bad news was about t' burst
As sadly we 'ad gone a bit to far -
For while a waitin' at the station
The Royal Gent 'ad come by car.
There was only a Miss Cawkell left
To entertain his 'ighness
Though I'm told she did the job so well
It cured for good - 'er shyness.

Alas the Royal anniversary -
Each year is not a big affair
It's not that the village 'as no pride
In fact we deeply care.
But we feels we should not put up
Marquees with fancy silks an' rugs
For Campden folk they might turn up
Just to see - ower red faced 'committee mugs'.

THE HIDCOTE CAT

GREENALLS

V.S.

The Hidcote Cat

Yubberton is a quiet place
Where most folk 'as a smilin' face,
But this 'asn't alus bin so
Cus they 'ad problems years ago -
Durin' the war - or just ater
There was a shortage o' water,
Most of the ditches adn't bin cleared
And a gret black rat 'ad just appeared.

A call went out for village men
To assemble at Righton's lambin' pen.
Where they was a listenin' to ol' Bill Payne
When - suddenly - it started to pour with rain.
"That's sorted the water," said 'is son 'arold
"Now lets sample one of Ol' Joe Page's barrels".
"We shouldn't stand out in this gloom
We should carry on in the assembly room".

A committee 'ad to be elected -
If these problems was to be corrected.
Bill Payne sat in the chair,
In the absence of the vicar - who wasn't there.
Son 'arold sat upon his right
An' Snooks to 'is left - what a sight.
Denny Proctor shouts, from behind a post,
"tis! Father, Son and Holy Ghost".

Bert Diston said 'e thought 'e knew
Just what Yubberton ought to do.
"Hidcote's got a thing so potent
That it could best your village rodent"
Bill Payne said "Bert there is a doubt
As to what You're a tellin' us about.
It's 'ard to believe there's somethin' that
Hidcote's got - can kill the rat".

The rat that was fust seen
Sittin' on the cricket green
Eatin' one of Stanley's lambs
Follered by a pair of Procter's hams.
It gave Roddy Emms such a fright,
Ended the cow charity, started by farmer Keyte
Caused chicken pox and infected
The Parish Council - just elected.

The villagers all agreed
That to 'idcote they must concede,
And give each of their men a wife -
Even to a free pint every day - for life.
Bert Diston and Jan the Pole
Left for a place they calls Cat 'ole,
It was a'ter dark and in the murk
When they returned to do their work.

There was no tellin' what was goin' on
But in the mornin' the rat was gone.
Snooks was of the view
The animal they'd used was from Peru.
'arold said "ere's what I thinks"
"They used a puma or a lynx".
"I dunno" said Bert, "if it's one like that -
We just calls it 'the 'idcote Cat!"

'arry's Teeth

'arry 'ad no trouble eatin'
'cos 'is teeth was all about,
Some on 'um still well-routed
Deep inside 'is gummy mouth.
But 'e still felt it was the time
That 'e should make a final will -
'cos 'e knew, that very soon,
'e'd 'ave to face the dentist's drill.

As 'e sat in the company of
Two dozen guppies in a tank,
'e thought of times gone past,
An' the people he must thank.
'is memories did calm 'im
As 'e sat there in reflection -
Till 'e saw the dentist was
A man of dark complexion.

107

'arry stammered 'e was sorry
For a wastin' of the dentist's time,
An' if 'e needed 'e'd be back,
But at the moment 'e felt fine.
'Is protests fell upon deaf ears
As the nurse sat 'arry in the chair.
"Open wide", were the dentist's words
Which began 'is worst nightmare.

The dentist found most teeth a missin'
And those left were very black
Except for one premolar
About 'alf way to the back.
The tooth puller was perturbed
At such lack of professional care -
But 'arry sez "I 'ave 'ad plenty
Of care - from round 'ere an' there"

The dentist asks ol' 'arry
To expand upon this wild claim,
While reasurin' 'im that 'e
Is not bein' 'eld to blame.
'arry sez "I 'as em pulled
By a mechanic in the garage,
'cos 'e's a man as cleans 'is pliers -
An' related to me by marriage.

The dentist 'ad to stop
An' consult 'is receptionist.
Who was well into 'er fifties
An' never 'ad bin kissed.
'e asked 'er if she could compare
With other men's mouths that she 'ad saw.
She snapped back - that she never 'ad
Looked in any man's mouth before!

The dentist stood an' pondered
The work that faced 'im yet,
So 'arry said, "do what yer can
An' I'll 'ave the rest done by the vet."
The dentist stood an' scowled,
Then 'is task, 'e set about
Which 'e completed by a pullin'
All of 'arry's teeth straight out.

Ol' 'arry's gums was sown
With catgut an' some string.
The dentist said "The lack of teeth
Will affect the way you sing."
'arry said " I 'aven't sung
For fifty years or so.
But with the faith that you've shown in me,
I'm be willin' to 'ave another go".

Then 'e thanked 'em all an' left,
with 'is pocket full of teeth.
At 'ome 'e took the mantel clock
An' 'id 'em underneath,
'Cos 'e would give 'is missus jewelry
For the first time in 'er life,
By 'avin' all 'is teeth made
Into a necklace for 'is wife.

The Yubberton Crow

Yubberton folk were oft disturbed
By a leghorn cock that crowed,
Every morning fair or foul,
Somewhere, up the 'idecote road.
Although they aired their views,
Outside the shop and moaned,
No-one was yet prepared to say,
If it was the one they owned.

Vigilante groups was formed
To seek out the raucous bird.
Milkmaids looked out for a cock
While a milkin' of the village 'erd.
Guardians left the parish gate
Used to shut the sunshine in
An' widows dressed in their black weeds
Searched all day for a drink o' gin.

The council felt the bird must go
So they put a price upon his 'ead -
Poultry, two and six a pound
With sauce from Tarplett's bread.
Many times did they pay out -
Money for the feathered shrieker -
But did refuse for one just plucked -
Described as a chicken streaker.

The weeks went by a pace
Till the weather was a getting' warm
An' the squire, 'e was attacked
By bees - from a Paxford swarm.
Nurse Joggins used 'er secret cure
For which she was paid a tanner.
But it's sweet smell just drew them bees
Right back into the Squire's Manor.

The council met outside
'Cause the days was very 'ot
An' the parish 'all 'ad just burnt down,
Which didn't 'elp a lot.
They made a declaration -
"All poultry would be rounded up -
An' to the man, 'andin' in that bird
They would give an 'almost silver' cup."

They called upon the band to play
To drown out the squarkin' bird,
But this just brought more trouble
With insomnia increasin' by a third.
An' a ring o' rabbits was seen to dance
A version of the Blakemore jig,
Causin' the drayman, an' 'is' orse
To crash their over loaded rig.

About this time a mystery
'Ad bin solved - right at the scene
Of the blockage in Mrs Stephen's drain
Now known caused by Ernie's runner bean.
A prize was given for it's length
With a speech that no-one 'erd,
 Cause the speaker, 'e was drowned out
By that rattlin' cockerel bird.

So all chicken's went by twelve bore -
Up to 'eaven for God to keep -
But the noise got worse an' worse,
Till there was no-one left asleep.
Then a wandrin' tramp was found -
A waitin' for the fruit to grow
'an with 'im was a mynah bird -
Right there unmasked as the 'Yubberton crow.'

Yubberton's Middlin' Engineer

Ol' Totty 'ad gone off to work
Just a couple o' weeks ago,
Where 'e was took quite bad
But with what 'e didn't know.
'e said, "I've got a sort of pain
But I'm not sure exactly where."
So they took ''im off to Asum
Cos the A & E was open there.

They rushed 'im into casualty
An wired 'im to an eltrocardiograph.
First they shaved 'is chest 'air off
Causin' ol' Tot to feel the draught.
The pain that started in 'is belly
'ad worked through to 'is back
Which gave the doctor cause to think
Ol' Tot 'ad 'ad an 'eart attack.

A mon who worked with Tot
Rang up an' told 'is missus,
"I "ave to say ol' Tot's bin took ill -
Which is in accordance with 'is wishes."
She was confused an' told the mon
"I don't believe a word of this from you
Totty would never wish to be ill -
Except for the occasional one day flu."

None the less she rang for a visit
But Asum said Totty wasn't there
He'd bin sent off to Worcester
To get some more intensive care.
Worcester though said, "'e's not 'ere,
We don't know where 'e was last seen
If 'e 'asn't got a bed in Asum
Perhaps 'e's somewhere in-between."

When they found out where 'e was
'is family went to visit 'im an' see
Why 'e was in the Alexandra as
It seemed the wrong place for 'im to be.
Totty said 'e didn't know till they 'ad said
And the news 'ad put 'im in a fluster
Cos all this time "e'd bin at Redditch
'e'd bin sure 'e was in Worcester.

Geoff and Rusty went to visit "im
An' asked "im what it was all about.
If 'e'd be kept in there for long
Or if 'e'd soon be comin' out,
Cos they 'ad to know - there an' then
Just 'ow much was 'e in pain
An' 'ow it would affect 'is drivin'
Cos they still 'ad them bikes to take to Spain.

He told 'em that when lay in bed
'e could 'ardly tell the pain was there
But every time he tried to work
It became far too much to bear.
Ol' Geoff said, "It's a great relief
That you're OK when lying flat
An' only "ave pain when your workin'
Cos you've always bin like that."

The doctors in the cardiac
Said Ol' Totty's heart was fine
An' 'is missus could take 'im 'ome -
If it would give 'er peace o' mind.
The sister said, "We need the bed,
You'll be fine as long as you don't bend
Because we can't cope with folk like you
Over a bank 'oliday weekend."

Ol Tot went 'ome in gret discomfort
An' couldn't eat a thing not greased with butter
So "is missus rang around the surgeries
Till she finally spoke to Dr. Lutter.
The doctor gave Tot's bowel a prod or two
Then muttered, "You need surgery I would say.
Take this note with you to Cheltenham
An' they'll admit you straight away."

The surgeon gave Ol' Tot a goin' over
Then 'e said, "You've not 'ad a 'eart attack
It's a blockage of the lower bowel
With inflammation in your digestive tract."
Well they'm goin' to do an' operation
But at least the national 'ealth be free
An' then what 'appens after that,
Well - we'll 'ave to wait an' see.

The Nameless Tree

I wrote to my orphanage
Where put when only three
For information held
To help me - with my family tree.
By return of post
I received a note
Upon which was wrote,
These few words to me.

Dear Sir or madam
This is all we know.
You came to us in a paper bag
With a label on your toe.
You were quite scanty clad
With no socks or shoes,
Wrapped in the weekly news -
Reporting a baby show.

We don't believe
That you were rejected
More an unpleasant surprise,
Turning up so unexpected.
It's clear from our records
You were put out alone
Both parents not known
And to date they're still undetected.

The note then concluded
All we have you've been shown
Though you're welcome to view files here
Or take them out on loan.
So I'll continue to search
For I can't let it be
While my family tree
Has so few leaves of her own.

Yubberton Tourism

The steam train now with empty tank
Struggled to climb up tunnel bank,
Ruinin' the railway's reputation
By giving up at Campden station.
The passengers had to disembark
Upon the platform - in the dark.
With nothin' left for them to do
They turned right from platform two.

Up the 'ill and round the bend
Then down to Yubberton they did descend.
The Vicar housed most of those people
In the nave an' up the steeple.
A few of them had to make a bed
Amongst the tools in Flimmy's shed.
Which was not so easily found
Due to Flimmy often movin' round.

Next day the guests stepped out of doors
Just as a bus appeared marked Larkin's tours.
The driver said "'tis two and nine -
Now the weather's turned out fine"
He went on to say, " without a map
What you needs most, is a trusty chap.
So this tour, it is a must
With a driver you can trust".

First stop was the Parish Church
Where they all began to search,
Fore signs of folk from long ago
Who tried to make the tower grow.
It's said they packed the muck real tight
So the walls would grow in height.
But no record did exist
So they turned in search of other myths.

But no one here could say at all
Which was Yubberton's famous wall
Where we're led to understand
The pig sat on, to watch the band.
Nor where the ring of stakes was put
In which they tried to shut,
The Cuckoo bird that wouldn't stay
But upped and went and flew away.

Ned drove off at such a pace -
As though 'e was out t' win a race.
Along past fields full a' ship
Down the gears through Water Grip.
Then out o' sight, no longer seen.
Past the farm at Battle Dean.
Through the bends at Puddlicot Mill
And back to Page's - up the 'ill.

They all went in the pub to take
A well earned rest an' dinner break.
Flimmy came in from Nibble n' Clink
Just for a draught of apple drink.
One or two looked 'im up an' down
An' decided 'e was the village clown.
So they set out to 'ave some sport
A usin' money to see 'im caught.

They'd offered 'im silver or some copper
Just to watch ol' Flimmy come a cropper,
By takin' the penny, for it was bigger
Which alus made them tourists snigger.
They would have a laugh and then
They 'd decide to trick 'im, once agen.
I asked Snooks why Ol' Flimmy was so daft.
He said, "It's practice Lad - an' a bit of craft."

At ten to 'leven ol' Joe called time -
Flimmy was up by 8/9d.
The Railway Company sent a bus
T' get them tourist's away from us.
They got in but paid the cost
For the driver said that 'e was lost.
So they 'ad to ask if we could say
In which direction was their way.

Harold said " I feel that, If you drove
Past the Hall, put up by Totty Grove
You would find the railway track.
Which alus 'elps, find your way back".
But Flimmy said, to their surprise,
"Let me give you some sound advice.
Unless you'm gooin' somewhere near
I'd advise you not to start from 'ere".

Paxford's Challenge

I met young Brian Wheatcroft
An' said "I'm off to Campden Town"
To which 'is smilin' face
Turned to one that wore a frown.
"Don't go over there," said 'e
"You can't trust they city dwellers
They'll 'ave the bread straight from your mouth
An' the cider from your cellars."

'e then went on to tell me
Of a challenge that was thrown out
Which 'ad caused the village problems
Of that, there was no doubt.
The band 'ad bin to Paxford,
Or so it was that 'e'd 'eard tell,
Where they was challenged to a contest
Which should include a choir as well.

Well, Yubberton 'ad bin without
Any sort of singing choir
Since the vicar 'ad some years ago
Stood trial - by ordeal of fire.
None of us knows what 'e'd done
For it's never come right out
But I 'eard a whisper once
T'was 'im as brought the plague about.

Now there was a girl at 'idecote
Who 'elped the squire's daughter,
To get over a swollen stomach
With a syringe an' some 'ot water.
Well, she could sing with any lark
And I was sure she'd 'elp us win,
But for the last three weeks or more
All 'idecote's bin snowed in.

Thank God for Malcolm 'aines
An' those other 'idecote men,
Who dug from early mornin'
To well after 'alf-past ten.
With very little left to drink
An' not a bite of warmin' grub
'til finally - they beat them drifts
An' arrived safely at the pub.

Them 'idecote men said she 'ad gone
Abroad, so it would seem,
But if we'em stuck then we should
Ask the Shipston rugby team.
Well them boys was very 'elpful
'cos they loves the singing of a song
So they agrees to be our choir
When Christmas comes along.

Upon Christmas Eve our band
Did in truth so sweetly play,
That the Paxford band threw in their hand
And Yubby won the day.
An interval was then taken
Which ended when ol' Joe Page,
Called on both the choirs
To come and take the stage.

Paxford sang their anthem
Worded just liked this;
"God bless our village girls
In cream dress and golden curls.
They wear long cloaks
Beneath the Paxford oaks
And sing songs of being pure
As they've always done before".

Our choir then sang in reply
Worded very much like this.
"God save their village girls
In a mess of tangled curls
Since a load of workin' blokes
Caught and trained by farmer Stokes
Taught them how to beg for more
In a way they'd never done before."

I can't explain exactly why
But I could very clearly sense,
That them assembled Paxford folk
'Ad took a gret offence,
About our choir's merry verse
With it's joyous well-sung lyric.
Perhaps it was the punches thrown-
Or just a lack of Christmas spirit.

Yubberton Water

Yubberton has a past so strange
As told by the farmer's daughter.
For our Health and wealth
Revolves around the water.
Pollution leads to many an ill,
Such as inlaws within the family
And harvests - just as poor
As those Reports of Farmer Stanley.

Spirits lives within the well
And comes up with the spring
Causes folk to say their prayers
And makes the Church bells ring.
Some vow a sheep laid eggs
And a calf was born to a Bull,
A donkey ate a wrought iron gate
On the night the Well was full.

Squire Bevington of the Manor
Had Campden's Rifles there
To carry out manoeuvres
And fire a volley in the air.
His Steward shouts they've missed,
The Captain said, "your lyin'"
But the truth is in the water
An' them pig's be still a flyin'.

Strange events would occur
At the slightest sign of rain
The foxes and the hares did bolt
As the hounds came off the train.
The broken trough at Hidecote
Created a big furore -
Sending Farmer Courtman's horse
And the Vicar off to war.

A Farm house near the well
Was in need of renovations -
So with plans drawn up in full
They sent out invitations,
To three bold Campden lads
Called Ticker, Pug and Ron
And a local they calls shady
Who were quickly taken on.

The job was to raise a lintel
And bed it way up high,
So they put their ladders up
In a perfect summer sky.
Then a gurgling from the well
Caused a great to do -
So gently they had hauled aloft
But that beam still split in two.

A local village farmer
Decided he would tell,
Why, when others failed
His crops had done so well.
"I asked the Squire's niece
If she would let me court her
An I lives along the Washbrook
But never drinks the water".

So let this grizzly tale
Be a lesson for all to see
Don't interfere with nature
The spirits must go free.
So we lets the water flow
To irrigate the farms
And does all of our drinking
In the bar of the Yubberton Arms.

Yubberton's Mounted Engineers

Ol' Totty bolts 'is shed door tight
And turns 'is back on Satd'y night
While a neighbour clearly 'ears 'im say
"Tomorrow's bound to be a better day".
Then farmer Stanley calls with a request
For which ol' Totty's men be suited best.
It is to return 'is new brood mare
By next day - to Paxford Livestock Fair.

Now Ol' Tot 'e needs some sound advice
Not 'avin' bin near a 'orse but twice.
So 'e calls to see Ol' Doug Cupper
Who's just sat down to eat a rabbit supper.
"Now Master Grove what can I do for 'e"
Tot sez, " I needs you to enlighten me.
For you've spent much time of course
A follerin' behind the workin' 'orse."

'E then explains the job 'e 'as been given
An' seeks to learn of Dougie's 'work-'orse livin'
Doug thinks for a while about Ol' Totty's plea
Then says, "I'll give all the 'elp I can to thee".
I'll take a short cut through Stanley's corn
An' be with you soon ater dawn.
Day break saw Doug an' 'is lad arrive
To 'elp them - an' the 'orse survive.

Doug sez, "'eaviest mon must take the 'ead
As these young mares are not so easy lead."
So Geof takes up 'is grip on 'er short rein
A mutterin', "I've got the bitin' end again."
"An'" sez Doug, "Totty, you must ride 'er there
While Rusty follers on in case of quick repair."
So Rusty takes a Whitworth spanner
An' 'is ol' pliers - with them to Paxford Manor.

They set's off across the field by Battle Dean
And quickly comes upon the live stock Queen -
A Paxford lass who seems in much distress,
A cardboard crown and low cut dress.
She asks them if they can kindly 'elp 'er out
Which they're keen to do - there is no doubt.
So Rusty 'elps 'er up to save 'er plight
While the mare gives Geof a crafty bite.

Ol' Tot tells Geof to walk on very slow
Towards the sound of Paxford show,
While in the saddle 'e an' the girl both settles
Not wishin' to fall into them nettles.
Rusty gives encouragement with a pat
Just as Geof steps into a slick cow splat
That causes 'is leadin' foot to slip
An' the mare to give 'im a nasty nip.

So Tot shouts, "Geof. now don't despair
For I'll swap with you when we gets there.
But alas just then the 'orse did buck
A throwin' Totty, an' the queen into the muck.
Rusty stands an' light's 'is pipe,
A stayin' clear of such an awful plight.
Sayin', "I can't 'elp out with such a mess
With these tools I can't mend a damaged dress."

Well that girl she was mostly nettle stung
With a coatin' of the meltin' dung -
While 'er regal dress was somewhat worn -
Some might say, 'quite badly torn.'
So she tells the lads where they can stick their aid
An' trudges off, a touch dismayed.
While the mare gives Geof a sudden jolt
As she struggles free an' starts to bolt.

Well, they arrives at Paxford feelin' ill
A'ter gettin' lost near Puddlicot Mill.
They follers the Queen in through the gate
As she apologised for 'erself a bein' late -
Sayin' she'd been attacked by cut-throats with a mare,
Resultin' in a need of 'first aid' care.
She's told the squire will offer a reward no doubt.
An' folks 'opes the police 'ave bin called out".

With one lost 'orse an' the squire livid.
Ol' Tot sees disaster loomin' over vivid -
While Goef 's preoccupied o' course
With the wounds 'e got, from that nigglin' - bitin' 'orse.
Rusty muses "'orses we can't understand
So we should leave 'em to them as works the land
And drink a fyow of them Paxford beers
For to quench we three - thirsty engineers."

Yubberton Independence

Yubberton folk were all agreed
The time had come to secede
From the rest of the English land
'cause of the tax put on their band.
A declaration of our new Realm
Was drawn up beneath the public Elm.
Then - from the steps of the Ol' Bake House
Read out by the niece of old Fred Rouse.

Bert Hawkins then set out to raise
Funds enough for a place to praise
This new Nation - who were bent
On forming their own Government.
In recognition of the proper job
Ol' Bert 'ad done, a raisin' many a bob'
It was decided that they would call
This fine new buildin', Albert's 'all.

The celebrations were all arranged -
Then of course some were changed.
Independence Day finally got under way
With a speech - a lunch an' a national play.
But while we all revelled in these happy scenes
Schemes were afoot to wreck our dreams.
An order was sent from the British Government
To put an end to Yubberton's upstart Parliament.

Ilmington responded to the Council's plan
They rallied round to a man,
Except of course for the odd defection,
In order to crush this insurrection.
They 'ad long been jealous of the way
Yubberton was always fust in makin' 'ay -
The pigs we raised upon the land
And of Yubberton's, prize winnin' band.

The Ilmington squire held a court
And decreed that all men should report
To the overseers and must conform
By reporting in some sort of uniform.
Three engine drivers arrived by van
Followed by an AA motorcycle man.
Then two postmen, advanced in years
And some Morris dancing fusiliers.

This army was the pride of the Stour valley
As dozens watched to see them rally.
Some wore Great Western railway caps
Some 'ad gaily coloured, 'untin' 'ats.
For they were dressed as a fighting force
And the Morris men wore bells of course.
Their weapons, supplied by Alfred Gault,
Were a set of darts - two bill'ooks and a catapult.

So they were ready by and large
But they needed a man in charge.
So they sorted out the ranks by wager,
The Morris fool became a Major.
A postman was promoted Quarter Master,
When the AA man had a 'bike disaster.
But the man in charge remains a riddle,
For they gave the job to the Morris Fiddle.

Battle commenced at the crack of dawn
Partly in a field o' corn
An' partly in a field o' new mowed 'ay
'Cause one o' the armies 'ad lost their way.
The fightin' it was very brief
Which was to farmer Keyte's relief
'Cause 'e was a man of religious whim -
An' both the fields belonged to 'im.

The matter was settled with a drink
Supplied, by a local plumber, so I do think.
'E gev Ilmington's army a drink called Diesel,
Smelt like a polecat an' bit like a weasel.
The drink was free so they drank their fill
Most o' them becamin' extremely ill !
So the Yubberton boy's raised their banner
On the roof of Ilmin'ton Manor.

The London government were not best pleased -
The Prime Minister stood an' wheezed,
"The whole episode's a complete disgrace
We've ended up with egg on our face.
Those people from some where in the west
Have cocked a snoop and come out best.
And now there's the gravest news of all -
I've been told they've stolen The Albert Hall!"

Amongst The Flowers

In memory of Diane Clarke 1948 - 2007

She was born – she stayed a while
And then was called to leave -
Leaving us a unique smile
In her own – no nonsense stile -
While declining the chance to grieve.

Once born she filled her time
In creative toil beyond dull grime -
Before her call to leave.
She - so deep in earnest to succeed
Had no time to grieve.

So passionate – she would spend hours
Among her own and other flowers
Tending - weeding through sun and showers
Until her time came to leave -
Leaving time for us to grieve.

But she was not born forlorn -
Though given cause to mourn
Before her time to leave -
We now are left with her legacy of hope
Amid our cause to grieve.

So we - in grief quietly bow
And hold that hope - closer now.